Bird Neighbour

Story by Wang Yanrong
Illustrations by Wu Daisheng

Zhaohua Publishing House
Beijing, 1984

Xiaoming lived with his grandfather in a cottage in the countryside. Every morning when his grandfather began work in the fields, Xiaoming went off to school.

He always passed a lovely old Chinese scholartree in front of their cottage. In the hollow of the tree lived a bird family: Father Bird, Mother Bird and their baby Little Spot.

Nobody knew how many generations of birds had lived next door to Xiaoming's family. Every morning, the birds awoke at dawn. They sang joyfully, announcing each happy day.

Father and Mother were never idle. They hopped about among the branches and busily ate worms.

When they were full, they brought food back for Little Spot. The young bird grew quickly. She was more beautiful than her parents, with her round head, sharp beak and a black spot at the top of her head.

The little bird soon grew big enough to join her parents when they searched for food. When they ate up all the worms in the Chinese scholartree, they flew to others. As they cleaned out the worms, all the trees in the area flourished and provided an ideal playground for the birds — they played hide-and-seek in the thick leaves.

One day when the sun was high in the sky, Mother Bird was combing her feathers. Father Bird and Little Spot were settling down for a nap. Suddenly something whizzed by them.

Father Bird became alarmed. He peered below him and saw the boy throwing stones at them.

The birds flew to the top branches of the tree. But they were not safe there either — the boy was aiming at them with a slingshot.

Father Bird thought it was an evil omen. He told Mother Bird and Little Spot, "It is dangerous to live here. Let's move somewhere else."

The birds' chirping ceased and as days passed by, the leaves became yellow and fell to the ground. Grandfather was puzzled. "Why are the leaves falling so early this year?" he murmured to himself.

One evening Xiaoming was eating his supper under the Chinese scholartree when a big worm fell into his bowl.

He was so frightened that he threw the bowl away and ran into the house, crying, "Grandpa, there are worms in the tree!"

Grandfather went out and examined the tree. Worms were wriggling all over the tree and the few leaves left were nearly eaten up.
"The tree will die unless it is sprayed with insecticide immediately," the old man sighed.

It was getting dark, but Grandfather seemed not to notice. He climbed up to the attic to look for the insecticide. Unexpectedly, he found many pebbles in the corner and a slingshot hanging on the beam.

Grandfather suddenly realized what had happend. He called Xiaoming and asked: "Xiaoming, can you tell me why the birds flew away?" "It's my fault," the boy answered in low voice. "I shot pebbles at them with my slingshot. They were frightened and flew away." He began to cry.

Grandfather then told Xiaoming: "Birds are friends of man. They not only sing beautiful songs but also catch worms. They helped the Chinese scholartree stay healthy and green."

Xiaoming made up his mind to correct his mistakes. Early each morning he crept under the tree and cheeped like a bird.

On his way to school, Xiaoming saw some birds eating worms. He made a detour in order not to disturb them.

When he saw other boys chasing birds, he told them to stop and explained why they should not hurt birds. Then he suggested some other games to play.

Time flew by and a year passed. Xiaoming became very skilful at imitating birds' songs. Many birds alit in the tree to listen to the beautiful sounds. Yet, they all flew away afterwards. Not one was willing to live in the old Chinese scholartree.

Xiaoming was disappointed. "Don't they believe my sincerity in correcting my errors?" he asked himself. Then one day, he saw a flock of birds wheeling in the air.

He recognized Little Spot by the spot on her head. Xiaoming was delighted. He chirped with all his might.

At the sight of Xiaoming, Little Spot was frightened again. "Is he going to hit us?" she asked Mother Bird.

"No," Mother answered. "Listen carefully. He is saying: 'I was wrong. I will never hurt you. Please come back to your native home.'"

Father Bird, Mother Bird and Little Spot, as well as some other members of their family moved back to their nest in the hollow. They cleaned their home and once again became Xiaoming's neighbour.

The expanded bird family feasted on the worms in the tree. It was not long before all the worms in the tree were **eaten** up.

Spring turned into summer. The healthy old Chinese scholartree was crowned with thick green leaves and laden with fragrant white flowers. The bird family chirped happily in its branches. Xiaoming was happy, too.

Publisher:

Zhaohua Publishing House
(A Subsidiary of China International Book Trading Corporation)
No. 21 Chegongzhuang Xilu, Beijing
China

Distributor:

China International Book Trading Corporation
(Guoji Shudian)
No. 21 Chegongzhuang Xilu
P.O.Box 399, Beijing
China